Investigating
CONTINENTS

ASIA

by Christine Juarez

raintree
a Capstone company — publishers for children

Raintree is an imprint of Capstone Global Library Limited, a company incorporated in England and Wales having its registered office at 264 Banbury Road, Oxford, OX2 7DY – Registered company number: 6695582

www.raintree.co.uk
myorders@raintree.co.uk

Designed by Cynthia Della-Rovere and Clare Webber
Picture research by Svetlana Zhurkin
Production by Kathy McColley
Originated by Capstone Global Library Ltd
Printed and bound in India

ISBN 978 1 4747 6110 9
22 21 20 19 18
10 9 8 7 6 5 4 3 2 1

British Library Cataloguing in Publication Data
A full catalogue record for this book is available from the British Library.

Acknowledgements
We would like to thank the following for permission to reproduce photographs:
Capstone Global Library Ltd, 5, 9; Shutterstock: Akkharat Jarusilawong, cover (bottom left), Alexander Mazurkevich, 17 (inset), creativestockexchange, cover (bottom right), back cover, 1, 3, DR Travel Photo and Video, cover (top), f11photo, cover (middle), John Haselman, 8, Michelle Cavanagh, 14, monotoomono, 19, Nelia redina, 17 (back), Sergey Uryadnikov, 15, stephen rudolph, 11, Tomasz Czajkowski, 7, Tony Duy, 21, trang trinh, 13, Wittybear (pattern), cover (left) and throughout

Every effort has been made to contact copyright holders of material reproduced in this book. Any omissions will be rectified in subsequent printings if notice is given to the publisher.

All the internet addresses (URLs) given in this book were valid at the time of going to press. However, due to the dynamic nature of the internet, some addresses may have changed, or sites may have changed or ceased to exist since publication. While the author and publisher regret any inconvenience this may cause readers, no responsibility for any such changes can be accepted by either the author or the publisher.

Contents

About Asia 4

Famous places 6

Geography 8

Weather 12

Animals 14

Plants 16

People 18

Natural resources and products 20

Glossary 22

Find out more 23

Comprehension questions 24

Index 24

About Asia

The world is made up of seven **continents**. Asia is the biggest continent. It starts near the Mediterranean Sea in the west and reaches the Pacific Ocean in the east. To the north is the Arctic Ocean. In the west is the continent of Europe. The Indian Ocean is south of Asia.

PACIFIC OCEAN

continent one of Earth's seven large land masses

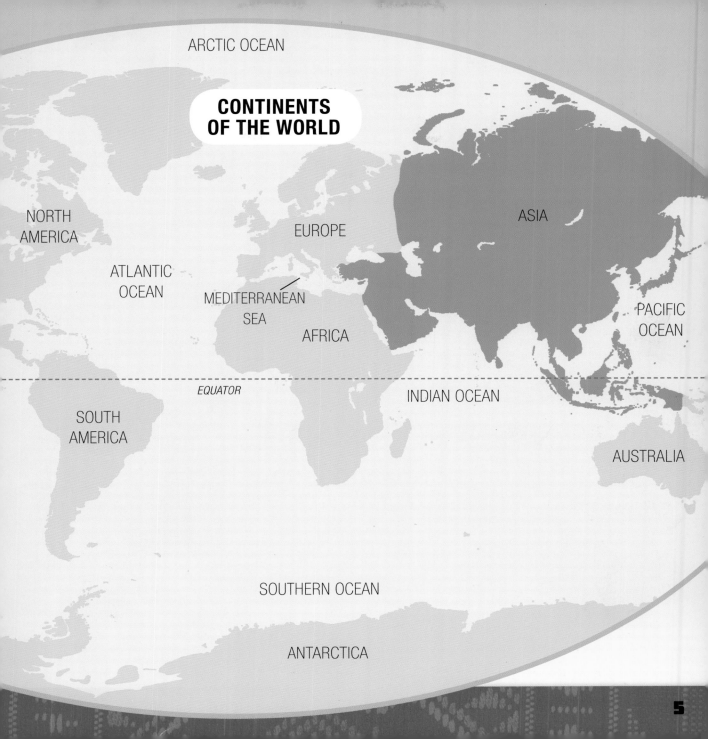

CONTINENTS OF THE WORLD

ARCTIC OCEAN

NORTH AMERICA

EUROPE

ASIA

ATLANTIC OCEAN

MEDITERRANEAN SEA

AFRICA

PACIFIC OCEAN

EQUATOR

INDIAN OCEAN

SOUTH AMERICA

AUSTRALIA

SOUTHERN OCEAN

ANTARCTICA

Famous places

Some of Asia's most famous places are very old. The Great Wall of China was built more than 2,300 years ago. The Taj Mahal in India was built more than 400 years ago.

Another famous place in Asia is **modern**. The Burj Khalifa in Dubai opened in 2010. It has 163 floors and is the world's tallest building.

The Burj Khalifa is in Dubai, United Arab Emirates.

modern up-to-date or new in style

6

Geography

Every type of landform is found in Asia. The Himalayas are the highest mountains on Earth. Mount Everest is the world's tallest peak. Huge deserts are found in Asia too. The rocky Gobi Desert is very hot in summer and very cold in winter. The Arabian Desert is found in western Asia. It connects Asia to the continent of Africa.

Mount Everest

Fact: Mount Everest is 8,850 metres (29,035) feet high.

Gobi Desert

Himalayas

Arabian Desert

Mount Everest

The longest river in Asia is the Yangtze River in China. It flows for 6,300 kilometres (3,915 miles) from the mountains in western China to the East China Sea. Millions of people live along the riverbanks.

Asia also has many lakes. The Caspian Sea is between Asia and Europe. It is the biggest lake on Earth. Although it is a lake, it is called a sea because it is salty.

Yangtze River

Weather

Asia is so big that it has all kinds of weather. In the far north, it is cold all year round. Southeast Asia is near the **equator** where it is always hot and wet. **Rainforests** grow well here.

Monsoon winds bring heavy rains to India and other countries. Some parts of Asia are hit by giant storms called typhoons. The strong storms cause flooding.

equator imaginary line around the middle of Earth

rainforest thick forest where rain falls nearly every day

Heavy rain causes streets to flood after typhoons.

Animals

Asia is home to amazing animals. Orangutans live in rainforests on the islands of Borneo and Sumatra. Komodo dragons are found in Indonesia. Giant pandas live in south-central China. They are very rare. There are fewer than 1,500 giant pandas left in the wild. There are so few because their forest homes are being cut down.

giant panda

orangutans

Plants

Asia has many different kinds of plants. Mangrove swamps grow along the coasts of India and Bangladesh. Mangroves are trees that have long roots. This helps them keep a firm hold in the mud. Pine, fir and larch trees grow all across northern Asia. Thick rainforests grow in Southeast Asia. One giant rainforest flower smells like rotting meat.

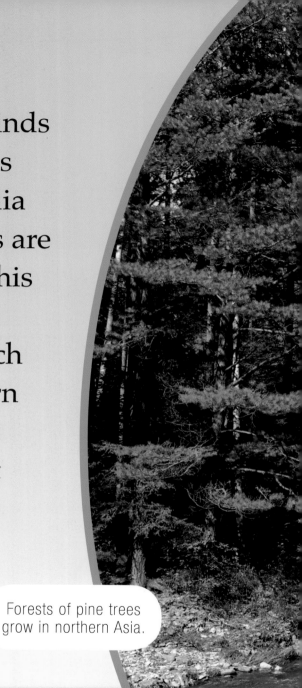

Forests of pine trees grow in northern Asia.

The rafflesia flower smells like rotting meat.

People

More than 4 billion people live in Asia's 48 countries. China and India have the most people. Many people live in small villages in the countryside. Cities in Asia are big and crowded. Shanghai in China, Mumbai in India and Tokyo in Japan are the biggest cities.

Thousands of languages are spoken in Asia. More than 1 billion people speak Mandarin Chinese.

Fact: The **population** of Asia is 4.5 billion people.

population number of people who live in an area

Mumbai, India

Natural resources and products

Asia's **natural resources** are in many different places. Oil is found in the Middle East. It comes from under the deserts. Countries in the Middle East sell oil all around the world.

Farms are found across Asia. Rice is grown in flooded fields. Wheat, cotton and tea are also grown in Asia. Many food products come from this continent.

natural resource material from nature that is useful to people

Workers pick tea leaves in a field in Vietnam.

Glossary

continent one of Earth's seven large land masses

equator imaginary line around the middle of Earth; it divides the northern and southern halves

modern up-to-date or new in style

natural resource material from nature that is useful to people

population number of people who live in an area

rainforest thick forest where rain falls nearly every day

Find out more

Books

Asia (Mathalon Maps), Joanne Randolph
(Raintree, 2017)

Living in China (Living in Asia), Annabelle Lynch
(Franklin Watts, 2016)

Mapping Asia (Close-up Continents), Paul Rockett
(Franklin Watts, 2016)

Websites

www.dkfindout.com/uk/earth/continents/asia/

Discover more about the wildlife and habitats of Asia.

www.natgeokids.com/uk/discover/geography/countries/facts-about-japan/

Learn more about Japan, including the fact that it is the only country in the world with a reigning emperor!

Comprehension questions

1. In which country do giant pandas live? Why are there so few giant pandas left in the wild?
2. What is the name of the highest mountains in the world? Where is the tallest peak found?
3. Name two of the biggest cities in Asia.

Index

animals 14

Burj Khalifa 6

cities 18

deserts 8, 20

farming 20

Great Wall of China 6

Himalayas 8

lakes 10

landforms 8

languages 18

Middle East 20

Mount Everest 8

natural resources 20

oceans 4

people 18

plants 16

population 18

rainforests 12, 14, 16

rivers 10

Taj Mahal 6

villages 18

weather 12